THE BIG BOOK OF CHRISTMAS SONGS

Available for

FLUTE, CLARINET, ALTO SAX, TENOR SAX, TRUMPET, HORN,
TROMBONE, VIOLIN, VIOLA, CELLO

T0084131

ISBN-13: 978-1-4234-1374-5

HAL•LEONARD®
CORPORATION
7777 W. BLUEMOUND RD. P.O. BOX 13819 MILWAUKEE, WI 53213

Visit Hal Leonard Online at
www.halleonard.com

ALL I WANT FOR CHRISTMAS IS YOU

VIOLA

Words and Music by MARIAH CAREY
and WALTER AFANASIEFF

A CAROLING WE GO

Music and Lyrics by
JOHNNY MARKS

Moderately bright

ALL MY HEART THIS NIGHT REJOICES

VIOLA

Words and Music by JOHANN EBELING
and CATHERINE WINKWORTH

Allegretto

ALL THROUGH THE NIGHT

Welsh Folksong

Moderately

ANGELS FROM THE REALMS OF GLORY

VIOLA

Words by JAMES MONTGOMERY
Music by HENRY T. SMART

Brightly

ANGELS WE HAVE HEARD ON HIGH

Traditional French Carol

Moderately

AS LONG AS THERE'S CHRISTMAS

from Walt Disney's BEAUTY AND THE BEAST - THE ENCHANTED CHRISTMAS

VIOLA

Music by RACHEL PORTMAN
Lyrics by DON BLACK

AS WITH GLADNESS MEN OF OLD

VIOLA

Words by WILLIAM CHATTERTON DIX
Music by CONRAD KOCHER

AULD LANG SYNE

Words by ROBERT BURNS
Traditional Scottish Melody

AWAY IN A MANGER

Traditional
Music by WILLIAM J. KIRKPATRICK

BRAZILIAN SLEIGH BELLS

VIOLA

By PERCY FAITH

Bright Samba

VIOLA

To Coda ⊕

BABY, IT'S COLD OUTSIDE

from the Motion Picture NEPTUNE'S DAUGHTER

VIOLA

By FRANK LOESSER

Moderately

BECAUSE IT'S CHRISTMAS
(For All the Children)

VIOLA

Music by BARRY MANILOW
Lyric by BRUCE SUSSMAN and JACK FELDMAN

AWAY IN A MANGER

Traditional
Music by JAMES R. MURRAY

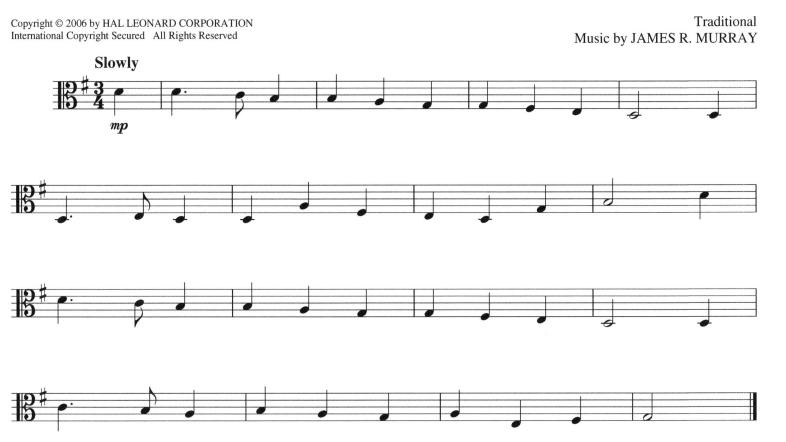

BLUE CHRISTMAS

VIOLA

Words and Music by BILLY HAYES
and JAY JOHNSON

BREAK FORTH, O BEAUTEOUS, HEAVENLY LIGHT

Words by JOHANN RIST
Melody by JOHANN SCHOP

THE BOAR'S HEAD CAROL

VIOLA

Traditional English

C-H-R-I-S-T-M-A-S

Words by JENNY LOU CARSON
Music by EDDY ARNOLD

20

BRING A TORCH, JEANNETTE, ISABELLA

VIOLA

17th Century French Provençal Carol

CAROL OF THE BELLS

Ukrainian Christmas Carol

CAROL OF THE BIRDS

Traditional Catalonian Carol

CAROLING, CAROLING

VIOLA

Words by WIHLA HUTSON
Music by ALFRED BURT

With a lilt

THE CHIPMUNK SONG

Words and Music by
ROSS BAGDASARIAN

Happily

A CHILD IS BORN IN BETHLEHEM

14th-Century Latin Text
Traditional Danish Melody

CHRIST WAS BORN ON CHRISTMAS DAY

Traditional

CHRISTMAS ALL ACROSS THE U.S.A.

VIOLA

Words and Music by
RITA ABRAMS

CHRISTMAS IN DIXIE

VIOLA

Words and Music by JEFFREY COOK,
TEDDY GENTRY, MARK HERNDON
and RANDY OWEN

CHRISTMAS IS ALL IN THE HEART

VIOLA

Words and Music by
STEVEN CURTIS CHAPMAN

Gently, in 2

CHRISTMAS IS

VIOLA

Lyrics by SPENCE MAXWELL
Music by PERCY FAITH

Slowly

CHRISTMAS STAR

from the Twentieth Century Fox Feature Film HOME ALONE 2

Words by LESLIE BRICUSSE
Music by JOHN WILLIAMS

Slowly, gently

CHRISTMAS TIME IS HERE
from A CHARLIE BROWN CHRISTMAS

Words by LEE MENDELSON
Music by VINCE GUARALDI

CHRISTMAS IS A-COMIN'
(May God Bless You)

VIOLA

Words and Music by
FRANK LUTHER

THE CHRISTMAS SONG
(Chestnuts Roasting on an Open Fire)

VIOLA

Music and Lyric by MEL TORME
and ROBERT WELLS

COLD DECEMBER NIGHTS

VIOLA

Words and Music by MICHAEL McCARY
and SHAWN STOCKMAN

THE CHRISTMAS WALTZ

Words by SAMMY CAHN
Music by JULE STYNE

Moderately, with expression

COME, THOU LONG-EXPECTED JESUS

VIOLA

Words by CHARLES WESLEY
Music by ROWLAND HUGH PRICHARD

Moderately

COVENTRY CAROL

Words by ROBERT CROO
Traditional English Melody

Gently

DANCE OF THE SUGAR PLUM FAIRY
from THE NUTCRACKER

VIOLA

By PYOTR IL'YICH TCHAIKOVSKY

DECK THE HALL

Traditional Welsh Carol

DO THEY KNOW IT'S CHRISTMAS?

VIOLA

Words and Music by M. URE
and B. GELDOF

Medium Rock

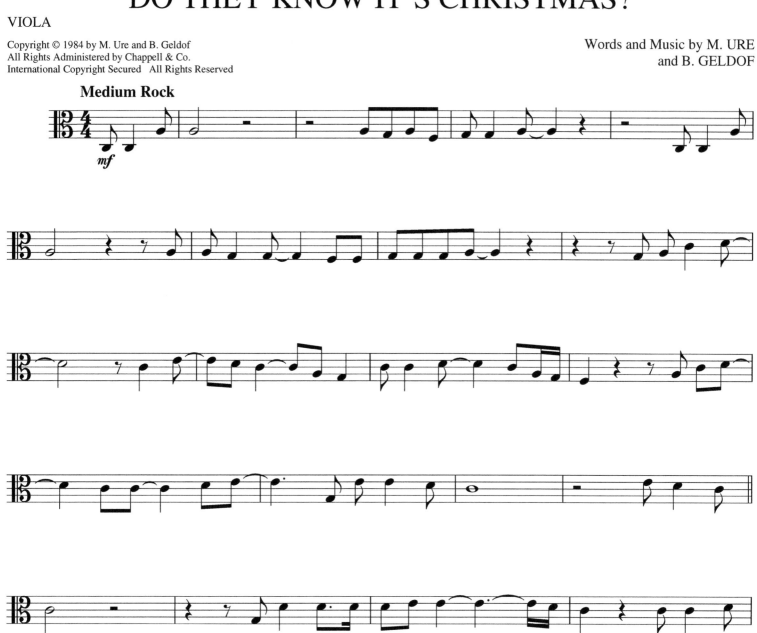

DON'T SAVE IT ALL FOR CHRISTMAS DAY

VIOLA

Words and Music by CELINE DION,
PETER ZIZZO and RIC WAKE

DING DONG! MERRILY ON HIGH!

VIOLA

French Carol

Moderately

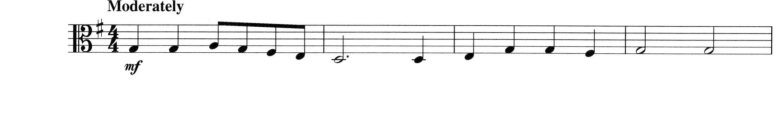

DO YOU HEAR WHAT I HEAR

Words and Music by NOEL REGNEY
and GLORIA SHAYNE

Moderately

To Coda

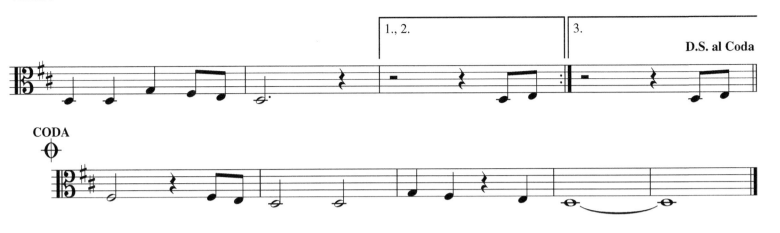

FELIZ NAVIDAD

Music and Lyrics by
JOSÉ FELICIANO

FROSTY THE SNOW MAN

VIOLA

Words and Music by STEVE NELSON
and JACK ROLLINS

THE FIRST NOEL

VIOLA

17th Century English Carol
Music from W. Sandys' *Christmas Carols*

THE FRIENDLY BEASTS

Traditional English Carol

FROM HEAVEN ABOVE TO EARTH I COME

Words and Music by
MARTIN LUTHER

THE GIFT

VIOLA

Words and Music by TOM DOUGLAS
and JIM BRICKMAN

Slow Ballad

GOING HOME FOR CHRISTMAS

VIOLA

Words and Music by STEVEN CURTIS CHAPMAN
and JAMES ISAAC ELLIOTT

Rhythmically and flowing

FUM, FUM, FUM

VIOLA

Traditional Catalonian Carol

GO, TELL IT ON THE MOUNTAIN

African-American Spiritual

GOD REST YE MERRY, GENTLEMEN

VIOLA

19th Century English Carol

GOOD CHRISTIAN MEN, REJOICE

14th Century Latin Text
14th Century German Melody

GOOD KING WENCESLAS

Words by JOHN M. NEALE
Music from *Piae Cantiones*

GRANDMA GOT RUN OVER BY A REINDEER

VIOLA

Words and Music by
RANDY BROOKS

GRANDMA'S KILLER FRUITCAKE

VIOLA

Words and Music by ELMO SHROPSHIRE
and RITA ABRAMS

Country Polka

THE GREATEST GIFT OF ALL

VIOLA

Words and Music by
JOHN JARVIS

Moderately slow

mf

HARK! THE HERALD ANGELS SING

Words by CHARLES WESLEY
Music by FELIX MENDELSSOHN-BARTHOLDY

GROWN-UP CHRISTMAS LIST

VIOLA

Words and Music by DAVID FOSTER
and LINDA THOMPSON-JENNER

HE IS BORN, THE HOLY CHILD
(Il est ne, le Divin Enfant)

Traditional French Carol

Brightly

GREENWILLOW CHRISTMAS

VIOLA

By FRANK LOESSER

HAPPY CHRISTMAS, LITTLE FRIEND

Lyrics by OSCAR HAMMERSTEIN II
Music by RICHARD RODGERS

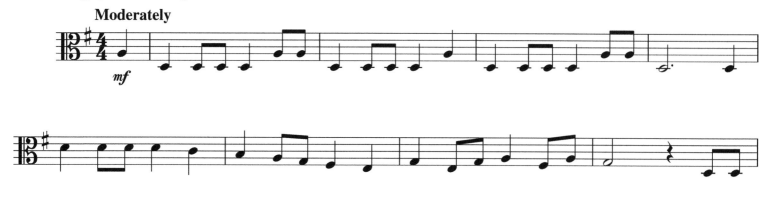

HAPPY HANUKKAH, MY FRIEND
(The Hanukkah Song)

VIOLA

Words and Music by JUSTIN WILDE
and DOUGLAS ALAN KONECKY

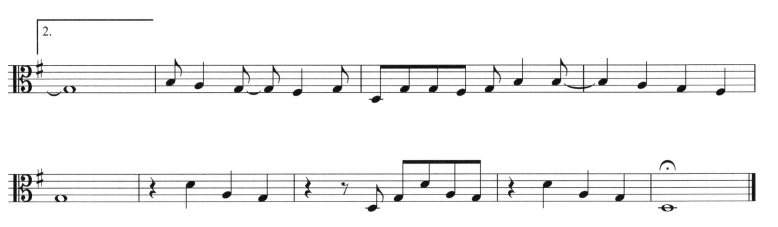

HAPPY HOLIDAY
from the Motion Picture Irving Berlin's HOLIDAY INN

Words and Music by
IRVING BERLIN

HARD CANDY CHRISTMAS

from THE BEST LITTLE WHOREHOUSE IN TEXAS

VIOLA

Words and Music by
CAROL HALL

HE

Words by RICHARD MULLEN
Music by JACK RICHARDS

HERE COMES SANTA CLAUS
(Right Down Santa Claus Lane)

Words and Music by GENE AUTRY
and OAKLEY HALDEMAN

HAPPY XMAS
(War Is Over)

VIOLA

Words and Music by JOHN LENNON
and YOKO ONO

HERE WE COME A-WASSAILING

VIOLA

Traditional

THE HOLLY AND THE IVY

18th Century English Carol

(There's No Place Like)
HOME FOR THE HOLIDAYS

VIOLA

Words by AL STILLMAN
Music by ROBERT ALLEN

Moderately

HYMNE

VIOLA

By VANGELIS

A HOLLY JOLLY CHRISTMAS

VIOLA

Music and Lyrics by
JOHNNY MARKS

I AM SO GLAD ON CHRISTMAS EVE

Words by MARIE WEXELSEN
Music by PEDER KNUDSEN

I HEARD THE BELLS ON CHRISTMAS DAY

VIOLA

Words by HENRY WADSWORTH LONGFELLOW
Music by JOHN BAPTISTE CALKIN

Moderately slow

I HEARD THE BELLS ON CHRISTMAS DAY

Words by HENRY WADSWORTH LONGFELLOW
Adapted by JOHNNY MARKS
Music by JOHNNY MARKS

Moderately

I SAW THREE SHIPS

Traditional English Carol

Brightly

I SAW MOMMY KISSING SANTA CLAUS

VIOLA

Words and Music by
TOMMIE CONNOR

I WONDER AS I WANDER

By JOHN JACOB NILES

I'M SPENDING CHRISTMAS WITH YOU

VIOLA

Words and Music by
TOM OCCHIPINTI

Moderately

I'VE GOT MY LOVE TO KEEP ME WARM

from the 20th Century Fox Motion Picture ON THE AVENUE

VIOLA

Words and Music by
IRVING BERLIN

Bright Jump tempo

I'LL BE HOME FOR CHRISTMAS

VIOLA

Words and Music by KIM GANNON
and WALTER KENT

Slowly

IN THE BLEAK MIDWINTER

Poem by CHRISTINA ROSSETTI
Music by GUSTAV HOLST

Moderately

IT MUST HAVE BEEN THE MISTLETOE
(Our First Christmas)

VIOLA

By JUSTIN WILDE
and DOUG KONECKY

Moderately

IT CAME UPON THE MIDNIGHT CLEAR

Words by EDMUND HAMILTON SEARS
Music by RICHARD STORRS WILLIS

IT'S BEGINNING TO LOOK LIKE CHRISTMAS

VIOLA

By MEREDITH WILLSON

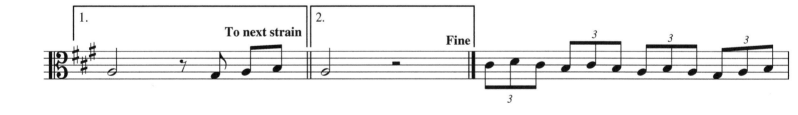

IT'S JUST ANOTHER NEW YEAR'S EVE

VIOLA

Lyric by MARTY PANZER
Music by BARRY MANILOW

IT'S CHRISTMAS TIME ALL OVER THE WORLD

VIOLA

Words and Music by
HUGH MARTIN

Fast and gaily

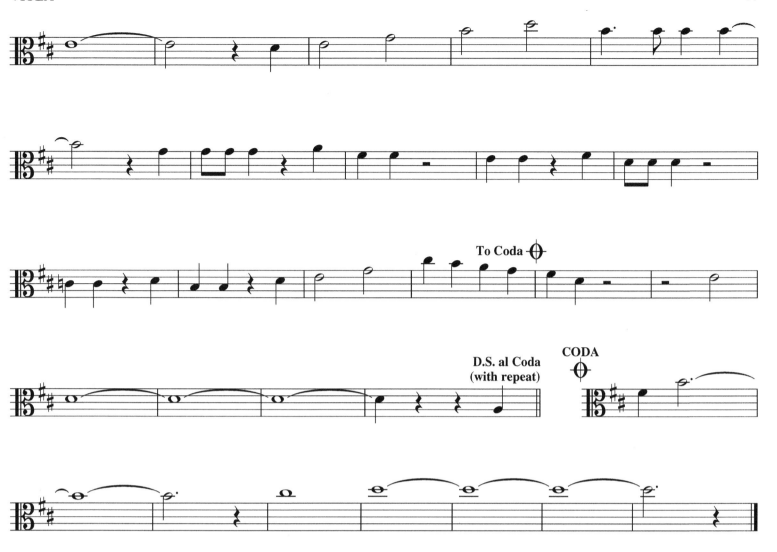

JESUS HOLY, BORN SO LOWLY

Traditional Polish

JESU, JOY OF MAN'S DESIRING

VIOLA

By JOHANN SEBASTIAN BACH

JINGLE BELLS

VIOLA

Words and Music by
J. PIERPONT

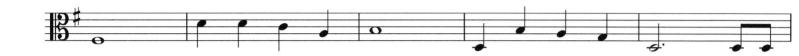

JINGLE, JINGLE, JINGLE

Music and Lyrics by
JOHNNY MARKS

JOLLY OLD ST. NICHOLAS

Traditional 19th Century American Carol

Moderately

JINGLE-BELL ROCK

VIOLA

Words and Music by JOE BEAL
and JIM BOOTHE

Moderately, with a Rock beat

LET'S HAVE AN OLD FASHIONED CHRISTMAS

VIOLA

Lyric by LARRY CONLEY
Music by JOE SOLOMON

LAST CHRISTMAS

VIOLA

Words and Music by
GEORGE MICHAEL

JOY TO THE WORLD

Words by ISAAC WATTS
Music by GEORGE FRIDERIC HANDEL

(Everybody's Waitin' For)
THE MAN WITH THE BAG

VIOLA

Words and Music by HAROLD STANLEY,
IRVING TAYLOR and DUDLEY BROOKS

LET IT SNOW! LET IT SNOW! LET IT SNOW!

Words by SAMMY CAHN
Music by JULE STYNE

THE LAST MONTH OF THE YEAR
(What Month Was Jesus Born In?)

VIOLA

Words and Music by VERA HALL
Adapted and Arranged by RUBY PICKENS TARTT
and ALAN LOMAX

LITTLE SAINT NICK

Words and Music by BRIAN WILSON
and MIKE LOVE

LO, HOW A ROSE E'ER BLOOMING

15th Century German Carol
Music from *Alte Catholische Geistliche Kirchengesang*

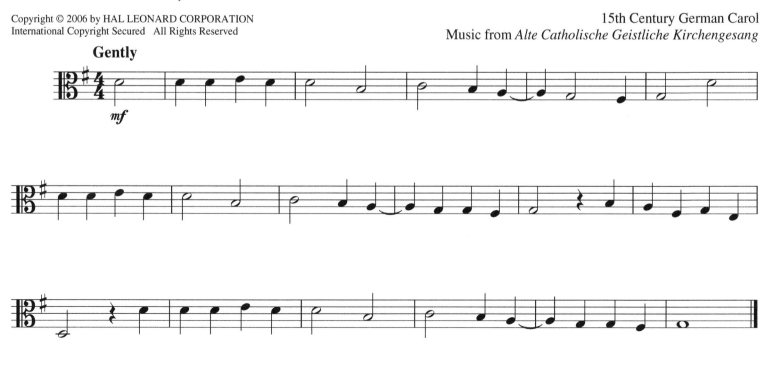

MARCH OF THE THREE KINGS

VIOLA

Words by M. L. HOHMAN
Traditional French Melody

March tempo

A MARSHMALLOW WORLD

VIOLA

Words by CARL SIGMAN
Music by PETER DE ROSE

With motion

MASTERS IN THIS HALL

VIOLA

Traditional English

MELE KALIKIMAKA

Words and Music by
ALEX ANDERSON

MERRY CHRISTMAS, BABY

VIOLA

Words and Music by LOU BAXTER
and JOHNNY MOORE

MERRY CHRISTMAS, DARLING

VIOLA

Words and Music by RICHARD CARPENTER
and FRANK POOLER

MERRY CHRISTMAS, MERRY CHRISTMAS

from the Twentieth Century Fox Feature Film HOME ALONE 2

VIOLA

Words by LESLIE BRICUSSE
Music by JOHN WILLIAMS

MISS YOU MOST AT CHRISTMAS TIME

VIOLA

Words and Music by MARIAH CAREY
and WALTER AFANASIEFF

THE MERRY CHRISTMAS POLKA

Words by PAUL FRANCIS WEBSTER
Music by SONNY BURKE

MISTER SANTA

VIOLA

Words and Music by
PAT BALLARD

A MERRY, MERRY CHRISTMAS TO YOU

Music and Lyrics by
JOHNNY MARKS

MISTLETOE AND HOLLY

Words and Music by FRANK SINATRA,
DOK STANFORD and HENRY W. SANICOLA

THE MOST WONDERFUL DAY OF THE YEAR

VIOLA

Music and Lyrics by
JOHNNY MARKS

THE NIGHT BEFORE CHRISTMAS SONG

Music by JOHNNY MARKS
Lyrics adapted by JOHNNY MARKS
from Clement Moore's Poem

Gaily

THE MOST WONDERFUL TIME OF THE YEAR

VIOLA

Words and Music by EDDIE POLA
and GEORGE WYLE

MY FAVORITE THINGS
from THE SOUND OF MUSIC

VIOLA

Lyrics by OSCAR HAMMERSTEIN II
Music by RICHARD RODGERS

Lively, with spirit

MY ONLY WISH THIS YEAR

VIOLA

Words and Music by BRIAN KIERULF
and JOSHUA SCHWARTZ

Fast Shuffle

O CHRISTMAS TREE

Traditional German Carol

O COME, ALL YE FAITHFUL
(Adeste Fideles)

VIOLA

Words and Music by JOHN FRANCIS WADE
Latin words translated by FREDERICK OAKELEY

Moderately

NUTTIN' FOR CHRISTMAS

Words and Music by ROY BENNETT
and SID TEPPER

Moderately bright

O COME, LITTLE CHILDREN

Words by C. VON SCHMIDT
Music by J.P.A. SCHULZ

Quietly

O COME, O COME IMMANUEL

VIOLA

Plainsong, 13th Century

Moderately

O LITTLE TOWN OF BETHLEHEM

Words by PHILLIPS BROOKS
Music by LEWIS H. REDNER

Slowly

O SANCTISSIMA

Sicilian Carol

Joyfully

O HOLY NIGHT

VIOLA

French words by PLACIDE CAPPEAU
English words by JOHN S. DWIGHT
Music by ADOLPHE ADAM

Moderately

OF THE FATHER'S LOVE BEGOTTEN

Words by AURELIUS C. PRUDENTIUS
13th Century Plainsong

Freely

ON CHRISTMAS NIGHT

VIOLA

Sussex Carol

OLD TOY TRAINS

Words and Music by
ROGER MILLER

PRETTY PAPER

Words and Music by
WILLIE NELSON

PLEASE COME HOME FOR CHRISTMAS

VIOLA

Words and Music by CHARLES BROWN
and GENE REDD

ONCE IN ROYAL DAVID'S CITY

Words by CECIL F. ALEXANDER
Music by HENRY J. GAUNTLETT

PAT-A-PAN
(Willie, Take Your Little Drum)

VIOLA

Words and Music by
BERNARD DE LA MONNOYE

RISE UP, SHEPHERD, AND FOLLOW

African-American Spiritual

ROCKIN' AROUND THE CHRISTMAS TREE

VIOLA

Music and Lyrics by
JOHNNY MARKS

Moderate Rock

RUDOLPH THE RED-NOSED REINDEER

VIOLA

Music and Lyrics by
JOHNNY MARKS

SANTA BABY

VIOLA

By JOAN JAVITS,
PHIL SPRINGER and TONY SPRINGER

Moderately slow

SANTA CLAUS IS BACK IN TOWN

VIOLA

Words and Music by JERRY LEIBER
and MIKE STOLLER

Slow Blues tempo

SANTA CLAUS IS COMIN' TO TOWN

Words by HAVEN GILLESPIE
Music by J. FRED COOTS

Moderate Swing

SHAKE ME I RATTLE
(Squeeze Me I Cry)

Words and Music by HAL HACKADY
and CHARLES NAYLOR

Moderately slow

SANTA, BRING MY BABY BACK
(To Me)

VIOLA

Words and Music by CLAUDE DeMETRUIS
and AARON SCHROEDER

Medium bright Rock

SHEPHERDS, SHAKE OFF YOUR DROWSY SLEEP

VIOLA

Traditional French Carol

With energy

SILVER AND GOLD

Music and Lyrics by
JOHNNY MARKS

Slowly and expressively

SILENT NIGHT

VIOLA

Words by JOSEPH MOHR
Translated by JOHN F. YOUNG
Music by FRANZ X. GRUBER

Slowly

SILVER BELLS
from the Paramount Picture THE LEMON DROP KID

Words and Music by JAY LIVINGSTON
and RAY EVANS

Moderately

SING WE NOW OF CHRISTMAS

VIOLA

Traditional French Carol

SNOWFALL

Lyrics by RUTH THORNHILL
Music by CLAUDE THORNHILL

SOME THINGS FOR CHRISTMAS
(A Snake, Some Mice, Some Glue and a Hole Too)

VIOLA

Lyric by JACQUELYN REINACH and JOAN LAMPORT
Music by JACQUELYN REINACH

Moderate Waltz tempo

SOME CHILDREN SEE HIM

Lyric by WIHLA HUTSON
Music by ALFRED BURT

SPECIAL GIFT

VIOLA

Words and Music by MYRON DAVIS
and STANLEY BROWN

SOMEWHERE IN MY MEMORY

from the Twentieth Century Fox Motion Picture HOME ALONE

Words by LESLIE BRICUSSE
Music by JOHN WILLIAMS

Gently and with simplicity

THE STAR CAROL

VIOLA

Lyric by WIHLA HUTSON
Music by ALFRED BURT

Tenderly, with much expression

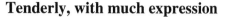

SUZY SNOWFLAKE

Words and Music by SID TEPPER
and ROY BENNETT

Moderately

TENNESSEE CHRISTMAS

VIOLA

Words and Music by AMY GRANT
and GARY CHAPMAN

STILL, STILL, STILL

VIOLA

Salzburg Melody, c.1819
Traditional Austrian Text

A lullaby

THAT CHRISTMAS FEELING

Words and Music by BENNIE BENJAMIN
and GEORGE WEISS

Slowly

THIS CHRISTMAS

VIOLA

Words and Music by DONNY HATHAWAY
and NADINE McKINNOR

TOYLAND

VIOLA

Words by GLEN MacDONOUGH
Music by VICTOR HERBERT

Slowly

mf

THE TWELVE DAYS OF CHRISTMAS

Traditional English Carol

Moderately

Verse 1

mf

Verses 2-4

*

Verse 5

Verses 6-12

*

These bars are played a different number of times for each verse.

UP ON THE HOUSETOP

VIOLA

Words and Music by
B.R. HANDY

WATCHMAN, TELL US OF THE NIGHT

Traditional

WE NEED A LITTLE CHRISTMAS

from MAME

VIOLA

Music and Lyric by
JERRY HERMAN

Brightly (as a Polka)

WE THREE KINGS OF ORIENT ARE

VIOLA

Words and Music by
JOHN H. HOPKINS, JR.

WE WISH YOU A MERRY CHRISTMAS

Traditional English Folksong

WEXFORD CAROL

VIOLA

Traditional Irish Carol

WHAT CHILD IS THIS?

Words by WILLIAM C. DIX
16th Century English Melody

WHAT ARE YOU DOING NEW YEAR'S EVE?

VIOLA

By FRANK LOESSER

Slowly and sentimentally

WHO WOULD IMAGINE A KING

from the Touchstone Motion Picture THE PREACHER'S WIFE

VIOLA

Words and Music by MERVYN WARREN
and HALLERIN HILTON HILL

Gentle Waltz

THE WHITE WORLD OF WINTER

Words by MITCHELL PARISH
Music by HOAGY CARMICHAEL

Moderately, with a lift

WONDERFUL CHRISTMASTIME

VIOLA

Words and Music by
PAUL McCARTNEY

YOU'RE ALL I WANT FOR CHRISTMAS

Words and Music by GLEN MOORE
and SEGER ELLIS

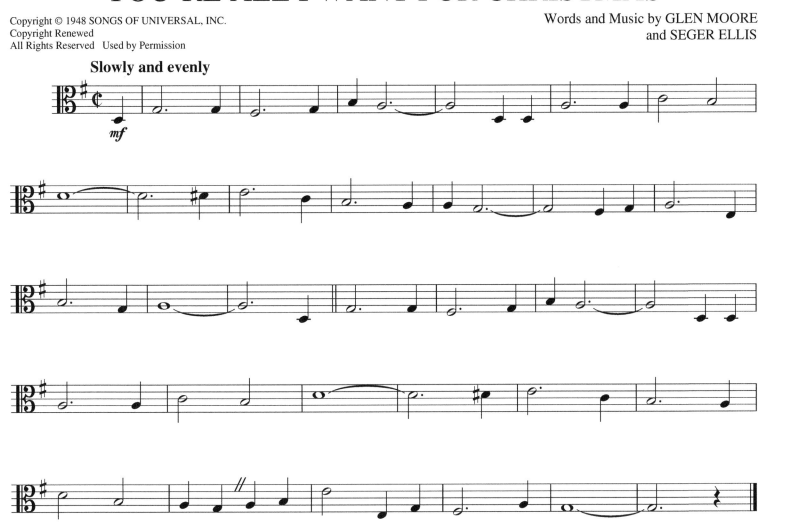

YOU DON'T HAVE TO BE ALONE

VIOLA

Words and Music by VEIT RENN,
JOSHUA CHASEZ and DAVID NICOLL

WHEN CHRISTMAS MORN IS DAWNING

Traditional Swedish

Moderately

144

WHEN SANTA CLAUS GETS YOUR LETTER

VIOLA

Music and Lyrics by
JOHNNY MARKS

Moderately